START EARNING WITH CHATBOTS- EVEN AS A BEGINNER!

HELLO
HOW CAN I HELP?
YOU LEFT SOMETHING IN YOUR CART
CHECKOUT NOW GET 10% OFF

+

CHATBOT

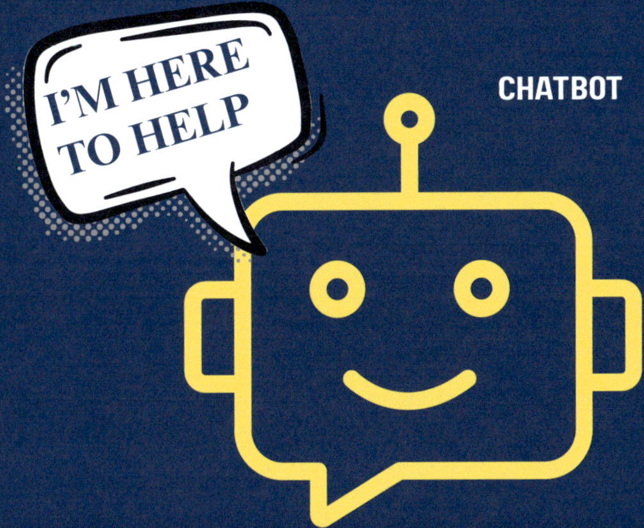

= AUTOMATION

= MORE FREE TIME DOING THE THINGS THAT YOU LOVE

CHATBOT GOLDMINE: A GUIDE TO MONETIZING CONVERSATIONS: PERFECT FOR NOVICE LEARNERS!

TANYA LOVEJOY-CAPERS

MONETIZE EVERY WORD: TURN EVERY CONVERSATION INTO A REVENUE OPPORTUNITY. WITH ACTIONABLE STEPS, DETAILED EXAMPLES, AND TIPS FOR SUCCESS, "CHATBOTS FOR PROFIT" IS YOUR GO-TO GUIDE FOR LEVERAGING THE POWER OF CHATBOTS TO BOOST YOUR BUSINESS'S BOTTOM LINE.

TANYA LOVEJOY-CAPERS

The TLC Touch Publishing, LLC
400 Gilead Road #2052
Huntersville, NC 28078

Chatbot Goldmine: A Guide to Monetizing Conversations Perfect for Novice Learners!

The information in this book is intended to be educational and does not provide any legal advice or directives about adversity or conflict with your institution. The content in this book is designed to be used as a supplement to the guidelines and policies prescribed by each institution. The author and publisher are not liable for any misuse of the material.

Paperback ISBN: 978-1-7355386-5-5

THIS GUIDE IS METICULOUSLY CRAFTED TO EMPOWER NOVICE INDIVIDUALS WITH THE TRANSFORMATIVE CAPABILITIES OF CHATGPT, OFFERING STEP-BY-STEP INSTRUCTIONS, TANGIBLE EXAMPLES, AND IN-DEPTH INSIGHTS TO REVOLUTIONIZE THEIR BUSINESS, ENSURING EFFICIENCY, PERSONALIZATION, AND SUCCESS IN EVERY TRANSACTION.

LET'S BEGIN YOUR JOURNEY INTO THE WORLD OF CHATBOTS

TABLE OF CONTENTS

TABLE OF CONTENTS

Preface

Welcome to "Chatbots Goldmine: A Guide to Monetizing Conversations." In the ever-evolving landscape of business, where technology intertwines seamlessly with human interactions, the role of chatbots has become increasingly pivotal. This guide is crafted with a singular purpose: to empower you, the reader, with the knowledge and strategies to turn conversations into a powerful engine for business success.

Why This Guide?

In a world inundated with information, my aim is clarity. The journey through the pages ahead is designed for both the curious novice and the seasoned entrepreneur looking to harness the potential of chatbots. Whether you're just dipping your toes into the waters of chatbot development or seeking innovative ways to monetize your existing conversational platforms, this guide is your companion.

Navigating the Conversational Landscape

The chapters ahead are not just informative; they are practical pathways into the world of chatbot mastery. Starting with the basics — understanding what chatbots are and their varied applications — I delve into the intricacies of designing effective bots. From selecting the right platforms to integrating artificial intelligence and machine learning, each step is a deliberate move toward enhancing your proficiency.

Monetization Unveiled

The heart of this guide lies in the exploration of monetization strategies. With clarity and actionable steps, I guide you through the process of turning conversations into revenue streams. Lead generation, e-commerce integration, subscription services, and affiliate marketing — each strategy is dissected, providing you with a comprehensive toolkit for success.

Real-World Wisdom

This guide is not just about theory; it's a repository of real-world examples and practical insights. Through case studies and success stories, I aim to spark your creativity and provide a blueprint for your own journey. The road to success is often paved with the experiences of those who ventured before us, and in these pages, you'll find valuable lessons learned from diverse industries.

Looking Beyond Today

The world of chatbots is dynamic, and as the technology evolves, so must our strategies. "Chatbots for Profit" doesn’t just focus on the present; it peers into the future. From augmented reality integration to voice-activated chatbots, we provide you with a glimpse of what lies ahead, ensuring that you're not just prepared for today's challenges but ready to seize tomorrow's opportunities.

Your Journey Starts Here

Whether you're an entrepreneur, a developer, or

an enthusiast eager to explore the vast potential of chatbots, this guide is your invitation to a journey of discovery and innovation. Let's embark together on a path where conversations aren't just exchanges of words but gateways to unprecedented business success.

Get ready to transform dialogues into dollars, and let the journey begin!

Warm regards,
Tanya Lovejoy-Capers

CHAPTER 1- INTRODUCTION

Welcome to the World of Chatbots

Welcome to an exciting journey into the world of chatbots! These intelligent programs bring technology and conversation to enhance customer experiences and open doors for businesses to generate revenue. Let us delve into the basics and explore how you can leverage chatbots to make your business thrive.

Definition of Chatbots

Chatbots, short for chat robots, are computer programs designed to chat with users, simulating conversation through text or voice interactions. Think of them as virtual assistants capable of understanding and responding to human-like queries. They have come a long way from basic rule-based systems to sophisticated agents with artificial intelligence (AI) that adapts and learns.

Rise of Chatbots in Business

More and more businesses are adopting chatbots to streamline communication, automate tasks, and offer instant support. This rise presents a golden opportunity for entrepreneurs and businesses to not just enhance interactions but also to monetize these conversations.

CHAPTER 2 – UNDERSTANDING CHATBOTS

Understanding Chatbots

Types of Chatbots:

Rule-based Chatbots

Imagine a chatbot following a set of predefined rules, like a script. These are rule-based chatbots, perfect for straightforward tasks where responses are predictable. For instance, a rule-based chatbot on a website guides users through a product catalog.

AI-based Chatbots

Now, picture a chatbot that learns and improves over time. These are AI-based chatbots, use machine learning and natural language processing. An example could be an AI-based chatbot in customer support, understanding and addressing user queries with growing accuracy.

Applications in Various Industries

Chatbots are not just for customer service. They play crucial roles in diverse sectors like e-commerce, healthcare, finance, and more. An e-commerce chatbot, for instance, could assist users in finding products, processing orders, and even offering personalized recommendations.

Voice-Activated Chatbots: Transforming User Interactions

Voice-activated chatbots, powered by technologies like speech recognition, offer a hands-free and intuitive interface. Users can engage in natural conversations with these bots, making them convenient for tasks like setting reminders, answering queries, or controlling smart home devices. The seamless integration of voice technology broadens the accessibility and user-friendliness of chatbots.

Multilingual Chatbots: Bridging Language Barriers

Multilingual chatbots are designed to understand and respond in multiple languages, breaking down language barriers for global audiences. Businesses with diverse customer bases can deploy multilingual chatbots to provide consistent and effective support, ensuring a seamless user experience regardless of language preferences.

Visual Recognition Chatbots: Enhancing Image-Based Interactions

Visual recognition chatbots leverage image recognition technology to interpret and respond to visual inputs. These bots find applications in various industries, from retail (helping users find products based on images) to healthcare (assisting in identifying medical conditions through images). The integration of visual recognition expands the scope of chatbots beyond text-based interactions.

Chatbots in Healthcare: Personalizing Patient Support

In the healthcare sector, chatbots are revolutionizing patient engagement. They provide personalized support by offering information about symptoms, medication reminders, and even monitoring chronic conditions. Healthcare chatbots contribute to improved patient outcomes by fostering consistent communication and adherence to treatment plans.

Legal Chatbots: Simplifying Legal Processes

Legal chatbots streamline legal processes by providing users with information about basic legal concepts, document preparation, and guidance on legal procedures. These bots empower individuals to navigate legal complexities more efficiently, offering accessibility and information crucial for informed decision-making.

Educational Chatbots: Enhancing Learning Experiences

Educational chatbots are transforming the way students learn by offering interactive lessons, quizzes, and personalized study plans. These bots adapt to individual learning styles, providing targeted support and additional resources. Educational chatbots contribute to a more engaging and effective learning environment.

Chatbots in Marketing: Personalizing Customer Interactions

In the realm of marketing, chatbots play a vital role in personalizing customer interactions. They analyze user preferences, behavior, and purchase history to offer tailored product recommendations, promotions, and assistance throughout the customer journey. Marketing chatbots contribute to increased customer satisfaction and conversion rates.

Marketing chatbots contribute to increased customer satisfaction and conversion rates by providing instant, personalized responses, guiding users through the sales funnel, and offering proactive support. They reduce wait times, answer common questions, and help customers find the right products or services, creating a seamless shopping experience.

Tangible Example: Retail Brand Boosting Sales with a Chatbot

Imagine Sarah, a busy professional, shopping online for a new pair of running shoes. She visits the website of FitStride, a popular athletic footwear brand. Instead of scrolling through hundreds of options, she interacts with StrideBot, the company's AI-powered chatbot.

StrideBot asks a few quick questions:

■ "What type of running do you do? (Road, Trail, Treadmill)"
■ "Do you prefer extra cushioning or a lightweight feel?"
■ "What’s your budget range?"

Based on her answers, the chatbot instantly recommends three top-rated running shoes that fit her needs. It also provides customer reviews, a comparison table, and an exclusive 10% discount code for first-time buyers.

Feeling confident in her choice, Sarah adds the shoes to her cart and completes her purchase—all within minutes.

Without the chatbot, she might have abandoned her search due to choice overload.

Key Impact:

- Higher Customer Satisfaction – Sarah received personalized recommendations without waiting for a human representative.
- Increased Conversions – The chatbot's tailored suggestions and discount incentive nudged her toward purchasing rather than browsing aimlessly.
- 24/7 Availability – Unlike human agents, StrideBot assisted anytime, helping customers shop at their convenience.

This example shows how marketing chatbots enhance customer experience, reduce friction in the buying journey, and ultimately boost sales.

Chatbots in Human Resources: Streamlining HR Processes

Human Resources (HR) chatbots streamline various HR processes, from employee onboarding and training to answering frequently asked questions. These bots enhance efficiency by providing quick responses and guidance, allowing HR professionals to focus on more strategic aspects of their roles. HR chatbots contribute to a more agile and responsive HR function.

HR chatbots are transforming human resources by automating repetitive tasks, ensuring seamless communication, and improving employee satisfaction. For example, during the onboarding process, a chatbot can guide new employees through essential steps such as submitting documents, understanding company policies, and setting up payroll preferences. Instead of waiting for an HR representative, employees receive instant, 24/7 support, reducing administrative delays and enhancing their overall experience.

Tangible Example:

Imagine a multinational company, Tech-Solutions Inc., that hires hundreds of employees each month. Managing onboarding manually led to inefficiencies, increased workload for HR staff, and delays in responses to new hires' inquiries. To solve this, they implemented an AI-driven HR chatbot named "HR Buddy (fictitious name)."

HR Buddy assists employees in multiple ways:

1. Automated Onboarding: It sends welcome emails, provides step-by-step guidance on document submission, and schedules introductory meetings.
2. Instant FAQ Support: Employees can ask HR Buddy about benefits, vacation policies, or expense reimbursement, and receive immediate, consistent answers.
3. Training & Development: The chatbot recommends relevant training programs based on job roles and tracks employee progress.

Impact: Within six months, Tech-Solutions Inc. (fictitious company) reduced onboarding time by 40%, cut HR inquiry emails by 60%, and saw higher employee engagement due to streamlined communication.

By integrating chatbots, HR teams can improve efficiency, reduce administrative burdens, and create a more employee-friendly experience, ultimately contributing to a more productive workforce.

Conclusion: Navigating the Diverse Landscape of Chatbots

Understanding the various types and applications of chatbots is crucial for navigating the diverse landscape of conversational AI. Rule-based chatbots excel in simplicity, AI-based chatbots evolve with complexity, and specialized chatbots cater to industry-specific needs. As the chatbot ecosystem continues to expand, businesses can leverage these diverse applications to enhance user experiences, streamline processes, and drive innovation across industries.

CHAPTER 3 – THE BUSINESS VALUE OF CHATBOTS

Improving Customer Service

Chatbots have become instrumental in revolutionizing customer service, offering swift responses, effective issue resolution, and seamless guidance to pertinent resources. Delving into specific examples showcases their impact on enriching customer interactions.

Quick Responses and Query Resolution:

Examples of How: A travel company utilizes a chatbot to promptly address booking inquiries and provide travel information. Users receive real-time responses, ensuring a smooth booking process.

Importance: Quick responses contribute to customer satisfaction, offering a seamless experience and fostering a positive perception of the brand's responsiveness.

Guidance to Resources:

Examples of How: A travel assistance chatbot doesn't just answer queries but guides users to relevant resources, such as travel guides or FAQs, ensuring users have comprehensive information.

Importance: Effective guidance enhances user self-service capabilities, reducing dependence on human support and empowering users with information at their fingertips.

Increasing Operational Efficiency: Streamlining Tasks for Business Agility

Automating routine tasks with chatbots is a strategic move to optimize operational efficiency, allowing human resources to focus on more complex activities. The transformative impact of chatbots is evident in various business functions, including human resources.

HR Chatbot for Employee Onboarding:

Examples of How: An HR chatbot streamlines the onboarding process by addressing FAQs, guiding new hires through paperwork submissions, and providing essential information.

Importance: Automating onboarding tasks enhances efficiency, ensuring a smoother transition for new employees and freeing HR professionals for more strategic responsibilities.

Routine Task Automation:

Examples of How: A finance chatbot automates invoice processing, expense tracking, and reimbursement procedures, reducing manual workload and minimizing errors.

homes but to help you make an informed decision every step of the way. This includes negotiating the best price, handling paperwork, and protecting you legally. If it's okay with you, I'd like to explain how our working relationship can make this journey smooth and enjoyable for you."

Why This Approach Works:

This response reassures the client by framing the realtor's role as an essential guide, not a salesperson. It educates clients on the importance of representation, setting up the expectation that the realtor is there to provide valuable expertise beyond simply showing homes.

Expected Positive Outcomes:

1. **Increased Client Trust:** By addressing their "just looking" mentality in a friendly, professional way, clients begin to view the realtor as a knowledgeable advocate.

2. **Enhanced Client Commitment:** By explaining the benefits of an agency agreement up front, clients are more likely to recognize the advantages of committing to a single agent.

3. **Stronger Collaborative Relationship:** This approach creates an atmosphere of partnership, establishing clear roles and expectations. As a result, clients are more likely to follow the realtor's recommendations and ultimately sign the agency agreement.

Importance: Automating routine tasks improves accuracy, reduces operational costs, and allows human resources to focus on tasks requiring creativity and critical thinking.

Interactive and personalized engagements are pivotal for fostering user engagement. Chatbots play a vital role in delivering tailored content and experiences that resonate with users, creating a more immersive and engaging environment.

Personalized News Updates:

Examples of How: A media outlet employs a chatbot to deliver personalized news updates to users based on their preferences, ensuring they receive content aligned with their interests.

Importance: Personalized content enhances user relevance and engagement, increasing the likelihood of user retention and satisfaction.

Exclusive Content Delivery:

Examples of How: A subscription-based chatbot service for a media outlet provides exclusive content, event notifications, and special offers to subscribers, creating a sense of exclusivity.

Importance: Offering exclusive content incentivizes user subscriptions, contributing to revenue generation while enhancing user engagement and loyalty.

Through these examples, the multifaceted contributions of chatbots in customer service, operational efficiency, and user engagement become apparent, illustrating their transformative impact across diverse business functions.

CHAPTER 4 - BUILDING AN EFFECTIVE CHATBOT

Selecting the Right Platform

In the vast landscape of digital communication, choosing the right platform for your chatbot is a critical decision that can significantly impact its effectiveness and reach. Each platform comes with its unique advantages, and understanding these distinctions is crucial for maximizing the potential of your conversational AI. Facebook Messenger, WhatsApp, and Slack stand out as prominent platforms, each offering distinct features that cater to specific business needs.

Consider Facebook Messenger, a juggernaut in the social media realm with unparalleled audience reach. Its expansive user base makes it an ideal choice for businesses aiming to connect with a broad demographic. The seamless transaction capabilities within Messenger further enhance its appeal, providing businesses, especially in the retail sector, with a versatile and widely used platform for customer interactions.

On the other hand, WhatsApp, with its focus on privacy and direct communication, is an excellent choice for businesses prioritizing one-on-one interactions. Its end-to-end encryption ensures secure communication, making it suitable for sensitive transactions or personalized customer support. Businesses looking to foster a more intimate connection with their audience may find WhatsApp to be the platform of choice.

Meanwhile, Slack positions itself as a collaboration hub, excelling in team communication and workflow management. While not as consumer-facing as Facebook Messenger or WhatsApp, Slack's strength lies in its utility for internal team interactions. Businesses emphasizing internal communication and task management may find Slack to be the ideal platform for integrating chatbots into their workflow.

Designing a Conversational Flow: Crafting Seamless Interactions

Once you've selected the platform, the next crucial step is designing a conversational flow that is not only natural but also user-friendly. Imagine a food delivery service's chatbot guiding users through the order process with clear and concise prompts. The key is to create a flow that mimics human conversation, making the interaction intuitive and enjoyable for users.

Start by mapping out the user journey, anticipating common queries, and designing prompts that guide users seamlessly through various processes. In the case of the food delivery service, the chatbot's prompts could include asking about the user's location, preferred cuisine, and any specific dietary preferences. Clear and straightforward language ensures that users can navigate the conversation effortlessly, enhancing their overall experience.

Utilizing decision trees and conditional logic can further refine the conversational flow, allowing the chatbot to adapt based on user responses. For instance, if a user expresses a preference for vegetarian options, the chatbot can tailor subsequent prompts and recommendations accordingly. Crafting a conversational flow is an iterative process, requiring regular testing and refinement to align with user expectations and business objectives.

Integrating AI and Machine Learning: Powering Continuous Learning

For AI-based chatbots, the journey doesn't end with the initial design; continuous learning is at the core of their functionality. Consider a language learning chatbot that adapts its responses based on user proficiency. This dynamic adaptation involves adjusting difficulty levels, providing targeted exercises, and even recognizing and correcting common mistakes made by users.

The integration of AI and machine learning enables chatbots to evolve with user interactions, becoming more adept at understanding context, nuances, and individual preferences over time. This capability is especially valuable in scenarios where personalization and tailored experiences are paramount, such as language learning or personalized recommendations in e-commerce.

Real-World Examples of AI & Machine Learning in Chatbots

- Language Learning Chatbot – Duolingo

Imagine Mark, who wants to learn Spanish. He uses a chatbot-powered language app like Duolingo, which adapts to his skill level. If he struggles with past tense verbs, the chatbot adjusts future lessons to reinforce that topic. Over time, it personalizes his learning path based on his mistakes and progress, making language acquisition smoother.

- E-commerce Recommendations – Amazon's Alexa

Lisa is shopping for skincare products on Amazon. She asks Alexa, "What's the best moisturizer for dry skin?" Over time, Alexa learns from her previous searches and purchases, suggesting brands and deals based on her preferences. This AI-driven personalization makes shopping more efficient and enjoyable.

- Music Streaming – Spotify's Chatbot

Jake uses Spotify daily and interacts with its AI-powered chatbot to request songs and create playlists. As he continues using the platform, the chatbot analyzes his listening habits and starts recommending songs that match his taste. Over time, it curates playlists automatically based on his mood and past behavior, enhancing his music experience.

Why This Matters

These examples highlight how AI-powered chatbots continuously learn and evolve, providing smarter, more personalized interactions that make everyday tasks—learning, shopping, and entertainment—more convenient and engaging.

The process begins with training the chatbot on a diverse dataset, exposing it to various language patterns, user queries, and potential scenarios. As users engage with the chatbot, it continuously refines its understanding, learning from successful interactions and adjusting its responses based on user feedback. This iterative learning loop ensures that the chatbot stays relevant and effective in delivering personalized and context-aware conversations.

In conclusion, selecting the right platform, designing a seamless conversational flow, and integrating AI and machine learning are pivotal steps in unleashing the full potential of chatbots. By understanding the strengths of each platform, creating user-centric conversational experiences, and harnessing the power of continuous learning, businesses can deploy chatbots that not only meet but also exceed user expectations, driving engagement and delivering value across various industries.

CHAPTER 5 - SELECTING THE RIGHT PLATFORM: NAVIGATING THE DIGITAL TERRAIN

Monetization Strategies: Unleashing the Revenue Potential

Embarking on the journey of chatbot monetization opens a world of possibilities. Let's delve into the exciting realm of making money with chatbots, exploring beginner-friendly strategies that can elevate your business's bottom line.

1. **Lead Generation: Guiding Toward Opportunities**

    - **Examples of How:** Start by designing conversation flows that ask users about their preferences and intentions, subtly guiding them toward relevant products or services. Picture an e-commerce chatbot engaging users in conversations about their style preferences, leading them seamlessly to personalized product recommendations.

    - **Importance:** By qualifying leads through chatbots, businesses can initiate meaningful interactions with potential customers, gathering valuable insights that lay the foundation for future conversions.

2. **Converting Conversations into Sales: Simplifying Transactions**

    - **Examples of How:** Make it easy for users to make purchases, bookings, or subscriptions directly within the chatbot. Implement secure payment gateways and optimize the checkout process for a seamless user experience. Imagine a travel agency's chatbot facilitating entire trip bookings within the conversation.

Temu is an excellent example of how streamlining the purchase process works.

How Temu Implements Seamless Purchases Through Chatbots

Temu, a fast-growing e-commerce platform, leverages AI-powered chatbots to create a frictionless shopping and checkout experience while also encouraging additional purchases before final order processing.

-Instant Product Recommendations & Guided Shopping

Temu’s chatbot engages users by suggesting relevant products based on their browsing history and preferences. For example, if a user searches for "wireless earbuds," the chatbot instantly recommends bestsellers, discounts, and customer reviews, guiding them toward a purchase.

- Seamless In-Chat Checkout

Once a user selects an item, Temu’s chatbot simplifies the checkout process within the chat interface, eliminating unnecessary steps. Instead of navigating through multiple pages, the chatbot:

1) **Automatically adds items to the cart**
2) **Provides payment options** (credit card, PayPal, Apple Pay, etc.)
3) **Offers real-time order tracking updates**
4) **This reduces friction and speeds up transactions, making it easier for customers to finalize their purchases.**

- **- AI-Driven Discounts & Upselling**

To maximize sales, Temu's chatbot suggests personalized upselling opportunities and discount offers. If a user buys a winter coat, the chatbot might recommend a matching scarf or gloves at a discount. Additionally, limited-time deals or coupons appear within the chat, increasing impulse purchases.

- Encouraging Additional Purchases Before Order Processing

A unique feature that Temu offers is the ability for customers to continue adding items to a recent purchase for a limited time before the final order is processed. The chatbot sends reminders such as:

1) "Still shopping? You can add more items to your order for the next 30 minutes!"
2) "Customers who bought [your item] also loved these! Add them before your order ships."

This encourages users to make last-minute additions, increasing the overall order value while maintaining a seamless experience.

Why This Matters

Temu's AI-driven chatbot mirrors the convenience of a personal shopping assistant, making transactions effortless while boosting average order value. By combining a frictionless checkout, AI-driven upselling, and a flexible purchasing window, Temu effectively maximizes conversions and customer satisfaction, setting a benchmark for chatbot-driven e-commerce.

- Importance: By streamlining the purchase process, businesses reduce friction in the customer journey, enhancing the likelihood of spontaneous conversions and fostering a positive perception of the brand.

3. E-commerce Integration: Personalized Recommendations

- Examples of How: Leverage AI algorithms to analyze user preferences and behavior, offering personalized product recommendations. Implement recommendation engines based on user history, preferences, and browsing behavior. Consider a chatbot from a tech retailer suggesting accessories based on a user's past purchases.
- Importance: Personalized product recommendations not only enhance user engagement but also increase the likelihood of conversion by presenting users with products that align with their preferences.

4. Streamlining the Purchase Process: In-Chat Convenience

- **Examples of How:** Allow users to complete transactions within the chatbot interface, implementing features like in-chat product browsing, order tracking, and one-click purchasing. Envision a food delivery service's chatbot seamlessly guiding users through menus, taking orders, and processing payments within the conversation.
- **Importance:** Streamlining the purchase process within the chatbot interface not only enhances user convenience but also accelerates decision-making, contributing to higher conversion rates.

5. Subscription Services: Exclusive Content Access

- **Examples of How:** Create subscription-based chatbot services offering exclusive content, updates, or benefits to subscribers. Develop a tiered subscription model with varying levels of access. Think of a news outlet's chatbot providing premium subscribers with early access to breaking news, exclusive interviews, and ad-free content.
- **Importance:** Subscription services capitalize on the allure of exclusivity, incentivizing users to subscribe for premium content, establishing a recurring revenue stream for businesses.

6. Premium Access through Chatbots: Elevated Experiences

- **Examples of How:** Offer premium services exclusively through the chatbot, defining features such as priority support, early access to new products, or exclusive content. Envision a fitness app's chatbot providing premium subscribers with personalized workout plans, direct access to trainers, and exclusive fitness tips —all accessed seamlessly through the chat interface.

- **Importance:** Premium access through chatbots enhances user experiences and provides an additional revenue stream for businesses, catering to users seeking heightened levels of service.

7. Affiliate Marketing: Strategic Integration

- **Examples of How:** Integrate affiliate links strategically into chatbot conversations, promoting products or services relevant to user inquiries. Partner with affiliate programs related to the chatbot's industry. Consider a travel chatbot incorporating affiliate links for hotel bookings or tour packages, earning commissions on successful referrals.

- Influencers can use chatbots to monetize their recommendations by strategically integrating affiliate links into their chatbot conversations. For instance, a beauty influencer could have a chatbot that interacts with followers and when users ask for skincare advice, the chatbot recommends products with affiliate links. Every time a user purchases a product through the chatbot's recommendation, the influencer earns a commission.

- Similarly, a fitness influencer could integrate affiliate links for workout gear or nutrition supplements directly into their chatbot interactions. If a follower inquires about protein powders or equipment, the chatbot could suggest items and seamlessly guide them to purchase. By partnering with affiliate programs related to their niche (e.g., beauty products, health supplements, travel gear), influencers earn commissions on each sale made through the links provided in their chatbot conversations.

- **Importance:** Affiliate marketing provides businesses with an additional revenue stream while offering users relevant recommendations, creating a symbiotic relationship between the chatbot and affiliate partners.

8- Tracking and Analytics: Informed Decision-Making

- **Examples of How:** Monitor the performance of affiliate links using tracking tools, regularly reviewing analytics to identify high-performing affiliate partnerships. An online shopping assistant chatbot could track affiliate link clicks and purchases, optimizing recommendations for better conversion rates.
- **Importance:** Tracking and analytics empower businesses to make data-driven decisions, refining monetization strategies based on performance insights and maximizing the effectiveness of affiliate marketing efforts.

9. **Data Monetization: Privacy-Driven Revenue**

- **Examples of How:** Maintain a strong commitment to user privacy, implementing robust data protection measures, obtaining user consent, and providing transparent privacy policies. A health and wellness chatbot collecting user information related to fitness routines must prioritize data security.
- **Importance:** Data monetization hinges on user trust. Ensuring privacy and ethical data practices not only safeguards user information but also fosters trust, a crucial element in successful data-driven revenue models.

10. Ethical Considerations: Balancing Profit and Principles

- **Examples of How:** Balance the desire for data monetization with ethical considerations. Regularly review data practices, seek feedback from users, and address concerns transparently. An educational chatbot should prioritize user consent and responsible data usage, ensuring a trust-based relationship with users seeking academic assistance.
- **Importance:** Upholding ethical considerations is integral for maintaining user trust, avoiding reputational risks, and fostering sustainable, long-term relationships with users. Ethical practices are a cornerstone of successful and enduring data monetization strategies.

In-depth discussions on these monetization strategies will follow, providing a nuanced understanding of each aspect, enabling businesses to navigate the complexities of chatbot monetization successfully.

CHAPTER 6 - CASE STUDIES

Let's explore how businesses across various industries are leveraging chatbot technology to drive growth, improve user engagement, and future-proof their operations. Each case study provides valuable insights, strategies, and practical takeaways that you can apply to your chatbot implementation.

1. Company A: Lead Generation Through Personalized Conversations

Challenge:
Generating and qualifying leads manually was time-consuming and ineffective.

Solution:
Company A deployed a chatbot that engaged users through a conversational quiz to identify their needs and product preferences. Based on responses, users were segmented and routed to appropriate sales reps or automated follow-ups.

Impact:
- 50% increase in qualified leads
- 70% reduction in manual lead screening time
- Improved lead-to-sale conversion rate by 22%

Key Takeaway:
Personalized, conversational lead qualification enhances user engagement

and improves the efficiency of the sales funnel.

2. Company B: Affiliate Marketing with Contextual Promotions

Challenge:
Company B wanted to monetize chatbot conversations without compromising user experience.

Solution:
They embedded affiliate links into chatbot conversations in a contextually relevant way, recommending products and services aligned with user queries or interests.

Impact:

- Generated $250K in affiliate revenue in 6 months
- Maintained high engagement (average session duration of 4.5 minutes)
- Increased affiliate link click-through rate by 40%
-

Key Takeaway:
The strategic placement of affiliate links within chatbot dialogues can create seamless, non-intrusive monetization opportunities.

3. Company C: Premium Access for Enhanced User Experiences

Challenge:
Differentiating service levels for free users vs. paying users was a top priority.

Company D: Successful Data Monetization Strategies

Case Study: Explore how Company D balanced data monetization with ethical considerations, ensuring user privacy while deriving value from data.

Key Takeaway: Ethical data practices are crucial for building trust, and user privacy should be a top priority in data monetization.

Solution:
Company C launched a chatbot-based premium access model, providing early updates, priority support, and exclusive tutorials to paying members via chatbot.

Impact:

- 2x higher satisfaction among premium users
- Premium upgrades increased by 33% in 3 months
- Help desk workload reduced by 25% through automated support

Key Takeaway:
Premium features delivered through chatbots can enhance perceived value, encourage upgrades, and improve support efficiency.

4. **Company D: Ethical Data Monetization Strategies**

Challenge:
Monetizing user data while complying with privacy regulations like GDPR (General Data Protection Regulation) and CCPA (California Consumer Privacy Act).

Solution:
Company D anonymized chatbot interaction data and created value-

added insights for partner brands, all while giving users transparent control over their data permissions.

Impact:

- Monetized data without a single privacy violation
- Gained industry recognition for ethical practices
- Improved user trust, reflected in a 95% satisfaction score

Key Takeaway:
Data monetization must prioritize ethics, transparency, and user consent to build long-term trust and avoid legal risks.

5. **Company E: Futureproofing with Advanced NLP**

Challenge:
Their previous chatbot struggled with understanding user context and intent.

Solution:
Company E implemented advanced Natural Language Processing (NLP) to improve the chatbot's ability to recognize sentiment, context, slang, and more nuanced queries.

Impact:

- User satisfaction improved by 60%
- Reduced misunderstanding rates by 70%
- Adapted to multiple languages and dialects

Key Takeaway:
Investing in advanced NLP enhances chatbot intelligence, making it more adaptable and future-ready.

6. **Company X: Boosting Sales with AI-Powered Product Recommendations**

Challenge:
Company X faced stagnating online sales and needed a way to better match products to customer preferences.

Solution:
They integrated an AI-driven chatbot capable of analyzing customer browsing history, previous purchases, and real-time user inputs. The chatbot would recommend products based on this behavioral data using machine learning algorithms.

Impact:

- 30% increase in average order value
- 25% higher conversion rates
- Reduced cart abandonment by 18%

Key Takeaway:
Understanding user behavior and leveraging AI to deliver personalized recommendations can significantly increase sales and customer satisfaction.

7. **Company Y: Subscription-Based Exclusive Content**

Challenge:
Company Y wanted to monetize its digital content while keeping engagement high.

Solution:
They introduced a subscription-based chatbot model that offered

exclusive articles, behind-the-scenes videos, and early access to releases. Subscribers received curated updates and content directly within the chat interface.

Impact:

- 40% increase in recurring revenue
- 3x higher user retention compared to non-subscribers
- Direct engagement increased by 60%

Key Takeaway:
Offering exclusive, high-value content through a chatbot builds loyalty and incentivizes users to subscribe, creating recurring revenue streams.

8. **Company Z: E-Commerce Integration & Streamlined Purchases**

Challenge:
Company Z needed to simplify its mobile shopping experience to reduce friction in the buyer journey.

Solution:
They fully integrated their e-commerce platform with a chatbot, allowing users to browse products, view reviews, add items to the cart, and complete purchases without ever leaving the chat window.

Impact:

- 45% faster checkout process
- 20% increase in repeat purchases
- Improved mobile conversion rate by 35%

Key Takeaway:
Integrating chatbot interfaces directly with e-commerce systems

improves user experience by streamlining purchases, boosting conversions, and customer satisfaction.

Lessons Learned from Across the Case Studies

1. **User-Centric Design:**
   Every successful case centered around understanding the user's needs, behavior, and preferences, then designing chatbot experiences to meet them.

2. **Seamless Integration:**
   Whether it's tying into e-commerce systems or CRM (Customer Relationship Management) platforms, Chatbots work best when they're part of a broader tech ecosystem.

3. **Monetization with Value:**
   Companies succeeded when chatbot monetization efforts (subscriptions, affiliate links, or premium access) added real value without compromising user experience.

4. **Ethical and Transparent Data Use:**
   Trust is earned by protecting user data and communicating transparently how it's used.

5. **Continuous Improvement:**
   Chatbots aren't a one-and-done solution. The best results came from ongoing testing, feedback, and adaptation.

6. **Futureproofing with Advanced Tech:**
   Technologies like NLP and AI recommendation engines allow chatbots to evolve with user expectations and industry trends.

CHAPTER 7 - CHATBOT ANALYTICS AND OPTIMIZATION IMPORTANCE OF ANALYTICS IN MONETIZATION

Dive into the significance of analytics in understanding user behavior, identifying trends, and optimizing chatbot performance.

Actionable Steps: Implement analytics tools to track user interactions, monitor conversion rates, and gather actionable insights.

A/B Testing for Improved Performance

A/B testing, also known as split testing, is a method used to compare two versions of a chatbot (A and B) to determine which one performs better. This technique helps in optimizing various elements of your chatbot to enhance user engagement and achieve your monetization goals.

What is A/B Testing?

A/B testing involves creating two versions of a chatbot, where one version (A) serves as the control and the other (B) introduces a specific change or variation. The goal is to compare how these versions perform against a predefined metric, such as conversion rates, user engagement, or revenue generation.

Actionable Steps:

1. **Identify a Specific Element to Test:**
   - Start with a clear hypothesis about which element of your chatbot you want to optimize. This could be the wording of responses, the placement of buttons, or the inclusion of specific features.

2. **Create Variations (A and B):**
   - Develop two versions of your chatbot: Version A, which remains unchanged (the control), and Version B, which includes the modification you want to test.

3. **Randomize User Exposure:**
   - Randomly assign users to either Version A or Version B. This helps ensure that your results are not biased by user characteristics.

4. **Collect Data:**
   - Implement analytics tools to collect relevant data on user interactions, conversions, or other key performance indicators.

5. **Analyze Results:**
   - Compare the performance of Version A and Version B based on the predefined metric. Look for statistically significant differences to determine the impact of the change.

6. **Implement Changes:**
    - If Version B performs better, consider implementing the changes into the main chatbot. If not, iterate and test other variations.

Example:

Let us say you are testing the effectiveness of a call-to-action (CTA) button in your e-commerce chatbot. Version A has the CTA button at the end of the conversation, while Version B introduces the CTA button earlier in the conversation. After running the A/B test, you find that Version B leads to a 20% increase in conversions. This insight allows you to optimize the chatbot by permanently moving the CTA button earlier in the conversation.

CHAPTER 8 - LEGAL AND ETHICAL CONSIDERATIONS: SAFEGUARDING USERS AND NAVIGATING REGULATIONS

Monetizing chatbots demands a responsible approach, balancing business objectives with ethical considerations and legal obligations. Navigating this landscape is critical for establishing trust with users and mitigating potential legal challenges.

Privacy Concerns and Compliance: Guarding User Data

Data Collection Transparency:

Examples of How: Clearly communicate what data your chatbot collects and how it will be used. Obtain user consent before collecting sensitive information. An e-commerce chatbot could explicitly inform users about data collection for order processing, ensuring transparency in the transaction process.

Importance: Transparent communication about data collection builds user trust, fostering a positive perception of the chatbot and the business it represents.

Compliance with Data Protection Regulations:

Examples of How: Familiarize yourself with data protection regulations such as GDPR (General Data Protection Regulation) or CCPA (California Consumer Privacy Act) and ensure that your chatbot complies with these standards. A finance chatbot, for instance, should adhere to strict data protection regulations when collecting financial information from users.

Importance: Compliance with data protection regulations is not just a legal requirement but also a commitment to user privacy, reinforcing trust and mitigating the risk of legal complications.

Secure Data Storage:

Examples of How: Implement robust security measures to protect user data from unauthorized access. Encrypt sensitive information and regularly update security protocols. A healthcare chatbot dealing with sensitive medical information must prioritize advanced encryption protocols.

Importance: Secure data storage not only safeguards user information from potential breaches but also assures users that their data is handled responsibly, contributing to a trustworthy user experience.

Transparency in Chatbot Interactions: Building Trust through Clarity

Disclose Bot Nature:

Examples of How: Inform users when they are interacting with a chatbot rather than a human agent. Transparency builds trust and manages user expectations. An insurance chatbot could openly state its

AI nature while providing assistance in processing claims.

Google's chatbot, like many advanced AI systems, excels at sound natural and human-like while interacting with users. It uses advanced Natural Language Processing (NLP) and machine learning algorithms to generate responses that mimic a real conversation. For example, if you're using Google's chatbot for customer service, it responds with a tone and cadence that closely resembles a human male, providing clear and natural responses to your inquiries.

In addition, Google's chatbot is highly intuitive, immediately understanding when you want to switch to a real person. If, at any point during the conversation, you express frustration or say something like, "I'd rather speak to a real person," the chatbot quickly recognizes your request and redirects the conversation to a human agent. This level of contextual understanding and seamless transition helps manage user expectations and ensures a smooth and efficient experience, building trust and confidence in the chatbot's capabilities.

For example, if you were dealing with an insurance chatbot, it might introduce itself by saying, "I'm an AI assistant here to help you with your claim today," ensuring transparency. However, if you then ask, "Can I speak with a real person?" the chatbot will promptly acknowledge your request and connect you to a human representative. This clarity and fluidity ensure that users feel they are in control of the experience.

Importance: Disclosing the chatbot's nature ensures transparency, preventing user confusion and fostering trust in the interaction, ultimately contributing to a positive user experience.

Provide Opt-Out Options:

Examples of How: Allow users to opt-out of data collection or disable certain features. Respecting user choices contributes to a positive user experience. A news chatbot might provide users with the option to opt-out of personalized news recommendations.

Importance: Providing opt-out options empowers users, respecting their preferences and reinforcing the user-centric approach, which is crucial for maintaining a positive relationship.

In-depth discussions on these legal and ethical considerations will follow, offering businesses insights into navigating the intricacies of compliance, fostering trust, and ensuring ethical practices in chatbot interactions.

CHAPTER 9 - FUTURE TRENDS IN CHATBOT MONETIZATION

Staying ahead of the curve involves anticipating future trends in chatbot technology and user expectations. As we look to the horizon, several exciting trends are set to shape the future of chatbot monetization.

1. Augmented Reality Integration:

One of the emerging frontiers is the integration of augmented reality (AR) into chatbots. Imagine a retail chatbot allowing users to virtually try on clothing items or visualize furniture in their own living spaces. AR-enhanced chatbots can revolutionize the way users engage with products, creating immersive shopping experiences.

Example:

Consider a home decor retailer incorporating AR into its chatbot. Users can virtually place furniture or decor items in their homes through the chatbot, helping them make more informed purchase decisions. This not only enhances the user experience but also increases the likelihood of successful conversions.

Importance:

Augmented reality integration provides a tangible and interactive dimension to chatbot interactions, creating memorable and personalized experiences for users. Businesses adopting AR-enhanced chatbots can differentiate themselves in the market, fostering customer engagement and loyalty.

2. **Voice-Activated Chatbots:**

Voice technology is advancing rapidly, and voice-activated chatbots are becoming more prevalent. The ease of interaction and hands-free nature make them particularly appealing. Picture a voice-activated assistant guiding users through a complex task or a voice-activated shopping assistant helping users place orders effortlessly. Integrating voice commands into chatbot interactions opens up new possibilities for user engagement.

Example:

A customer service chatbot in a smart home device company could be voice-activated, allowing users to troubleshoot issues or set up their devices through voice commands. This streamlined and intuitive interaction enhances the overall user experience.

Importance:

Voice-activated chatbots cater to users who prefer spoken interactions, providing a more natural and convenient way to engage with technology. This trend is significant for accessibility and inclusivity, expanding the reach of chatbots to a broader audience.

3. **Advanced Natural Language Processing (NLP):**

Advancements in Natural Language Processing (NLP) are propelling chatbots to better understand context, sentiment, and nuances in user conversations. Future chatbots equipped with advanced NLP capabilities can engage in more natural, human-like conversations. This evolution is essential for providing personalized and context-aware responses, enhancing user satisfaction.

For example, in a Google Assistant commercial, a person asks their phone, "Hey Google, what's the weather like today?" After receiving the answer, they follow up with, "Will it rain later?" The assistant responds smoothly, demonstrating its ability to handle follow-up questions without needing restarts, mimicking the flow of a real conversation. Later, the person asks, "Can you remind me to call mom at 5 PM?" and the assistant confirms, showcasing its ability to seamlessly switch between tasks.

What makes this commercial stand out is that the assistant doesn't just answer in a robotic tone; it engages in natural, fluid exchanges as if conversing with a real person. This highlights how Google's chatbot technology can understand context, interpret nuances, and respond in a way that feels like a genuine human interaction, allowing users to have a full conversation with it.

A Deeper Dive into Natural Language Processing NLP?

Advanced Natural Language Processing (NLP) refers to the sophisticated and intricate capabilities of natural language processing systems that go beyond basic language understanding. NLP is a subfield of artificial intelligence (AI) that focuses on the interaction between computers and human language. Advanced NLP involves more complex and nuanced language comprehension, allowing machines to understand context, sentiment, and subtle nuances in human communication.

Here are some key characteristics and features of advanced NLP:

Contextual Understanding: Advanced NLP systems can understand the context in which words and phrases are used. This includes recognizing references, maintaining context across sentences, and comprehending the broader meaning of a conversation.

Sentiment Analysis: These systems can analyze and interpret the sentiment expressed in text, identifying whether the language used is positive, negative, or neutral. This is crucial for understanding user emotions and responding appropriately.

Named Entity Recognition (NER): Advanced NLP includes NER capabilities, allowing the system to identify and classify entities mentioned in the text, such as names of people, locations, organizations, dates, and more.

Syntactic and Semantic Analysis: Beyond basic language structure, advanced NLP delves into syntactic and semantic analysis, understanding the relationships between words, the meaning of phrases, and the overall structure of sentences.

Coreference Resolution: This involves the ability to resolve references in a text, such as identifying when "he" or "it" refers to a specific person or object mentioned earlier in the conversation.

Pragmatic Understanding: Advanced NLP systems aim to understand not just the literal meaning of words but also the implied meaning, sarcasm, humor, and other pragmatic aspects of communication.

Multilingual Capabilities: Some advanced NLP models can process and understand multiple languages, breaking down language barriers and providing a more inclusive user experience.

Continuous Learning: Advanced NLP systems may incorporate machine learning techniques, enabling them to adapt and improve over time based on the data they receive and the interactions they have.

In summary, advanced NLP represents a higher level of sophistication in language understanding for machines, allowing them to engage in more human-like and context-aware conversations. This is particularly valuable in applications such as chatbots, virtual assistants, sentiment analysis, and other natural language processing tasks.

Example:

An advanced customer support chatbot with enhanced NLP can discern user frustration and tailor its responses accordingly. It can offer empathy and solutions more effectively, improving the overall customer service experience.

Importance:

Advanced NLP ensures that chatbots can comprehend and respond to users in a manner that aligns with human communication. This results in a more meaningful and effective interaction, contributing to increased user satisfaction and engagement.

4. Chatbots in Virtual and Augmented Reality Spaces:

Imagine a future where chatbots seamlessly integrate into virtual and augmented reality spaces. Users could interact with chatbots in virtual environments, enhancing collaboration, training, or entertainment experiences. Businesses may employ chatbots in VR meetings, guiding users through information or assisting in real-time problem-solving.

Example:

In a corporate training scenario, an HR chatbot could guide employees through a virtual onboarding process, providing information and answering questions within the immersive VR environment.

Importance:

The integration of chatbots into virtual and augmented reality spaces extends their utility beyond conventional platforms. This opens up opportunities for innovative applications in training, collaboration, and entertainment, creating unique user experiences.

5. **Integration with Wearable Devices:**

As wearable technology continues to evolve, chatbots are expected to integrate seamlessly with devices like smartwatches and augmented reality glasses. Users could receive personalized notifications, access information, or engage in conversations directly through their wearable devices. This hands-free accessibility expands the reach and convenience of chatbots.

Example:

A fitness chatbot integrated with a smartwatch can provide real-time workout guidance, track progress, and offer fitness tips—all without the need for users to pull out their smartphones.

Importance:

Integration with wearable devices enhances the accessibility of chatbots, allowing users to engage in conversations and access information conveniently on the go. This trend aligns with the growing prevalence of wearable technology in daily life.

6. Emotional Intelligence Integration:

The future of chatbots includes advancements in emotional intelligence integration. Chatbots may evolve to recognize and respond to user emotions, adapting their tone and responses accordingly. This humanizes the interaction, making chatbots more empathetic and capable of providing tailored support based on user emotions.

Example:

A mental health support chatbot with emotional intelligence capabilities can detect signs of distress in users' messages and respond with empathy and encouragement, providing valuable emotional support.

Importance:

Emotional intelligence integration enables chatbots to understand and respond to users' emotional states, fostering more compassionate and personalized interactions. This contributes to a higher level of user trust and satisfaction.

As we navigate the exciting terrain of future chatbot trends, businesses that embrace these advancements will be better positioned to deliver exceptional user experiences and unlock new avenues for monetization. Stay informed, adapt to these trends, and explore the possibilities that the future holds for chatbot technology.

CHAPTER 10 - TIPS FOR SUCCESS

Monetizing chatbots demands an adaptive approach, recognizing the fluid nature of technology and user preferences. As you embark on this transformative journey, here are four additional tips to guide your chatbot towards sustained success:

1. **Embrace Continuous Learning:**

    - In the rapidly evolving landscape of chatbot technology, staying abreast of the latest advancements is imperative. Regularly engage with industry forums, attend webinars, and explore emerging technologies. This ensures your chatbot remains at the forefront of innovation, offering users cutting-edge features and experiences.

2. **User Feedback Integration:**

    - User feedback is a goldmine of insights that can fuel the evolution of your chatbot. Establish channels for users to provide feedback, whether through in-app prompts or dedicated feedback forms. Actively analyze this feedback and incorporate valuable suggestions into your chatbot's development roadmap. Users appreciate platforms that listen and respond to their needs, fostering a sense of partnership.

1. **Scalability Planning:**

    - Anticipate and plan for scalability as your chatbot gains popularity. A sudden surge in user interactions or data volume should not compromise the chatbot's performance. Regularly assess the infrastructure's scalability and optimize resources to accommodate increasing demands. This proactive approach ensures a seamless user experience, even during periods of heightened activity.

2. **Agile Iterations and Updates:**

    - Adopt an agile development approach that facilitates rapid iterations and updates. Users appreciate chatbots that evolve with their needs and preferences. Implement a release schedule that introduces new features, refines existing functionalities, and addresses any identified issues. Agile iterations not only keep your chatbot dynamic but also showcase a commitment to continuous improvement.

Sustained success in chatbot monetization requires a holistic and forward-thinking strategy. By embracing continuous learning, integrating user feedback, planning for scalability, and adopting agile development practices, your chatbot can navigate the ever-changing landscape, consistently delivering value to users and contributing to your business's bottom line.

Integration of Proven Practices:

1. **Regularly Evaluate Performance:**

   - Conduct regular reviews of your chatbot's performance using analytics data. Identify areas for improvement and iterate on the design.

1. **Stay Informed About Industry Trends:**

   - Keep abreast of industry trends, technological advancements, and changes in user behavior to adapt your chatbot strategy accordingly.

Listening to User Feedback:

1. **Encourage User Feedback:**
   - Actively seek feedback from users to understand their experiences and expectations. Use this feedback to make informed adjustments to your chatbot.

1. **Responsive to User Needs:**
   - Be agile in responding to user needs and concerns. Flexibility and responsiveness contribute to a positive user experience.

CONCLUSION

In the dynamic landscape of chatbot monetization, the key lies in understanding your users, optimizing your chatbot's performance, and staying attuned to industry trends. By implementing the strategies and tips outlined in this guide, you can unlock the full potential of chatbots as a revenue-generating tool for your business.

Conclusion: Unlocking the Potential of Chatbot Monetization

In the ever-evolving realm of chatbot monetization, success hinges on a trifecta of principles: understanding users, optimizing performance, and aligning with industry trends. This comprehensive guide has navigated through the intricacies of turning conversations into revenue, offering a roadmap for businesses to harness the full potential of chatbots.

Understanding Users:

The journey begins with a profound comprehension of chatbots, those AI-driven virtual assistants designed to simulate human-like conversations. From their humble rule-based origins to the sophisticated AI-powered agents of today, the rise of chatbots in various industries has opened up unparalleled opportunities for businesses to not only enhance interactions but also generate substantial revenue.

Optimizing Chatbot Effectiveness:

Exploring the nuances of chatbot applications across diverse sectors—from e-commerce and healthcare to finance and beyond—reveals their multifaceted roles as virtual assistants, sales representatives, and information providers. Delving into the intricacies of designing effective chatbots, this guide provides insights into selecting the right platform, crafting natural conversational flows, and integrating AI and machine learning for continuous improvement.

Monetization Strategies Unveiled:

The heart of the guide lies in monetization strategies, offering a nuanced exploration of lead generation, e-commerce integration, subscription services, affiliate marketing, and data monetization. From designing conversation flows that qualify leads to seamlessly integrating transactional capabilities, businesses can leverage chatbots for personalized product recommendations, streamlined purchase processes, exclusive content delivery, premium access, affiliate marketing, and responsible data monetization.

Real-World Insights:

Embarking on a journey of real-world examples, this guide unveils successful applications across industries. Companies like Company X and Company Y serve as beacons, showcasing how AI-driven recommendations and subscription-based chatbot models can significantly impact sales and user engagement.

Ethical Considerations and Privacy:

As the guide delves into ethical considerations and user privacy, it emphasizes the delicate balance required for data monetization. Case studies illustrate the importance of maintaining user trust through transparent data practices and a commitment to ethical considerations. Examples span across sectors, from finance to health and wellness, showcasing the critical role of user trust in successful data monetization.

Continuous Improvement and Success Tips:

To ensure sustained success, the guide concludes with tips encompassing continuous learning, user feedback integration, scalability planning, and agile iterations. By staying informed about industry trends and listening to user needs, businesses can adapt and thrive in the dynamic landscape of chatbot monetization.

In summation, this guide is a comprehensive handbook, equipping businesses with the knowledge and tools to transform their chatbots into not just conversational partners but robust revenue engines. By understanding, optimizing, and staying ahead of the curve, businesses can unlock the full potential of chatbots, propelling them into a new era of customer engagement and financial success.

RESOURCES

Explore the following tools, platforms, and learning materials to further enhance your knowledge and skills in chatbot development and monetization. (*The resources are mere suggestions, and you must keep in mind that with evolution in technology, information is prone to rapidly change as new advances are implemented*)

Recommended Tools and Platforms

- Chatbot Development Platforms: A list of platforms to help you build and deploy chatbots.
- Analytics Tools: Tools for tracking and analyzing user interactions with your chatbot.

Further Reading and Learning Materials

- Books on Chatbot Monetization: A curated list of books to deepen your understanding of chatbots and monetization strategies.

Recommended Books:

1. "Designing Bots: Creating Conversational Experiences" by Amir Shevat
    - This book focuses on designing effective conversational experiences and is suitable for both beginners and experienced developers.
2. "Chatbots: An Introduction and Easy Guide to Making Your Own" by Matthew Harper

    - Geared towards beginners, this book provides a hands-on guide to creating chatbots without the need for extensive programming knowledge.
3. "Conversational Design" by Erika Hall
    - While not specifically about chatbots, this book delves into the principles of designing effective conversations, which is crucial for chatbot development.

Online Courses:

- **Enroll in courses to enhance your skills in chatbot development, AI, and machine learning.**

Online Courses

1. **Coursera: "Building Conversational Experiences with Google Dialogflow"**
    - This course, offered by Google Cloud, covers the fundamentals of building conversational agents using Google's Dialogflow platform.
2. **Udemy: "Chatbot Building: Develop a Chatbot with No Coding"**
    - Geared toward beginners, this Udemy course teaches the basics of chatbot development without requiring extensive coding skills.
3. **edX: "Microsoft Professional Certificate in Artificial Intelligence"**
    - This comprehensive program by Microsoft covers various aspects of AI, including natural language processing, which is essential for chatbot development.

4. **LinkedIn Learning: "Learning Chatbot Development with Microsoft Bot Framework"**
    - This course focuses on building chatbots using Microsoft's Bot Framework, making it suitable for developers interested in Microsoft technologies.

Additional Resources:

1. **Chatbot Platforms Documentation:**
    - Explore the documentation of popular chatbot development platforms such as Dialogflow, Microsoft Bot Framework, and Rasa. These resources often provide in-depth tutorials and guides.
2. **GitHub Repositories:**
    - **Many developers share their chatbot projects on GitHub. Exploring these repositories can provide practical insights and examples.**

Remember to check the latest reviews and ratings for online courses and verify if there are more recent books or courses available, as the field of chatbot development is continuously evolving.

YOUR NOTES:

YOUR NOTES:

YOUR NOTES:

YOUR NOTES:

YOUR NOTES:

YOUR NOTES:

YOUR NOTES:

YOUR NOTES:

YOUR NOTES:

YOUR NOTES:

YOUR NOTES:

YOUR NOTES:

YOUR NOTES:

YOUR NOTES:

Made in the USA
Monee, IL
05 November 2026

67988163R00050